Judy,
you have the Power.
Joan Kennedy

NOW

or

NEVER

THE CHOICE IS YOURS

JOAN KENNEDY

ISBN: 978-1-946195-22-7

Library of Congress Number: 2017962375

21 20 19 18 17   5 4 3 2 1

Contact: Joan Kennedy joan@joankennedy.com

Editing: Connie Anderson:
WordsandDeedsInc.com

Cover Design: Allan Pranke: AMP13.com

Page Setup: Ann Aubitz:
Fuzionprint.com
Published by: FuzionPress
1250 E 115th Street
Burnsville, MN 55337

TODAY
IS NOT JUST ANOTHER
DAY...
IT'S YOUR LIFE!

Dedication

To my children, Bob, Marnie,
Patty, and Amy, who bring joy
and unconditional love to my heart.

Acknowledgments

I would like to extend my deepest thanks and appreciation to a number of people who made a special contribution with their ideas and insights.

My special thanks to my daughter, Amy Kennedy Fosseen, who gave me the idea for the book. I also want to thank her for all her help, encouragement and for her joyous manner, while helping me.

A special thanks to my daughter Patty Kennedy Bronstien, for the first editing, her suggestions and personal involvement in the book. Thank you for taking the time out of your busy schedule to help me.

My thanks to Connie Anderson, the final editor of the book. I also want to thank her for her willingness to share ideas that added a great dimension to the book.

Contents

Introduction | 11

Preface | 17

Your Power Source | 19

It's at the Core of Your Being | 37

A Method of Change | 51

Dream Big! Think Big! Set a Big Goal | 65

Fear Stops You in Your Tracks | 89

Visualize What You Want | 101

A Self-Fulfilling Prophesy | 111

About the Author | 135

Book Order Form | 138

NOW *or* NEVER

Introduction

For years my marriage had fluctuated between feelings of frustration and contentment. When I was frustrated, I took down walls, moved furniture, and changed my kitchen curtains. When I was content, I cleaned, washed windows and kept an orderly house, like any other sane housewife would do.

During the years that I was married and raising my children, I was forever busy. The decorating, remodeling and all my other busy work were an escape. I was avoiding the real conflicts within myself and my life. My marriage was crumbling. I had no future in terms of marketable skills. I was forty-five, with three children at home, little work experience, and no money of my own.

While I was married, I was never concerned with looking for a job, or preparing myself for one, either mentally or emotionally. I had no expectations of working outside my home. I saw no need for any further planning. I thought I had reached my major goal in life: the role of wife and mother. I didn't want to make any drastic changes, but after the divorce, I had to.

A feeling of fear would grip me each time I considered giving up my familiar ways and accepting the challenge of the unknown. The thought of undertaking anything as monumental as getting a job was frightening.

After many financial setbacks, I finally decided to look for a job. But with my sketchy work experience, the thoughts that kept surfacing were, "What can I possibly do?" and "Who'd want me?" It was clear to me no one would hire me because I was just a housewife. Many times I asked myself, "How could I have spent so many years on this earth, and not end up with something I could do to make a living."

Prior to my marriage, I was a fashion model and worked in a fashion office downtown St. Paul. Now, I discounted the possibility of getting a job in fashion because I thought I was too old.

At a friend's suggestion, I applied for a job at the University of Minnesota. Along with my application, I was told I had to take a Civil Service test. After completing the tests,

Joan Kennedy

I had to wait in the hallway for my test results.

After some time, the personnel manager finally came out of his office and walked over to me. He didn't take me into his office as he had done with everyone else. He said, "Mrs. Kennedy, you passed your tests, but you don't know how to do anything." Well, *I knew that when I left home in the morning.* Now he knows it, and everyone within earshot knows that I don't know how to do anything. I don't remember my answer, if any. All I remember is the embarrassment I felt. He then said, "We have a part-time job at Nicholson Hall Bookstore." Although the job was for two weeks out of each quarter, I jumped at the opportunity—I finally had a job. Later, I found out it was part-time because the job didn't require a Civil Service test. To work at Nicholson Hall Bookstore, one just had to be ambulatory.

The job was far from challenging, and it didn't provide me with an adequate income. For the extra money, I worked for my friends; work I was capable of doing, like washing walls, painting, refinishing furniture, mending Oriental rugs, and cleaning houses. Needless to say, some of the jobs did

NOW *or* NEVER

little for my self-image. In the past, I found that when things really became difficult, something always presented itself. However I always looked to others for the solution to my situation, not realizing I had within myself powerful resources to solve my own problems.

When I was trying to change my circumstances, I started reading self-help books. One of the books I picked up at our library was *Psycho Cybernetics* by Dr. Maxwell Maltz. Although, at the time, I didn't know what the title meant, our librarian knew I was interested in reading self-help books, and told me it was a good book. I began reading, and I knew that I had to buy my own book because *Psycho Cybernetics* was not going to be a quick read. As I started reading, everything started to make sense. Months later, after reading the book several times, and following the techniques he laid out, I asked myself again, "What can I do?" "What talents do I have to offer?" This time when my experiences as a model surfaced, instead of thinking, "Who'd want me?" Something had changed. I felt differently about myself. Now, I could truthfully say, "Why not me?" It didn't seem ridiculous to try to get back

Joan Kennedy

into the fashion business. For the first time, I knew in my heart I could do it.

I called to schedule an interview with a fashion director at one of the leading department stores in Minneapolis. I was given an appointment for the following month. From that point until the day of the interview, I visualized the interview. I went over in my mind all the various questions the fashion director would ask me. One of the interesting part of the book was when Dr. Maxwell Maltz writes about the power of our imagination. He said, "Mental pictures offer us an opportunity to practice new traits and attitudes, which otherwise we could not do. This is possible because our nervous system cannot tell the difference between an actual experience and one that is vividly imagined." Each night, after I got into bed, I would completely relax my body. I would then rehearse the interview, in my mind, and every night, as I pictured the interview, the fashion director would say, "You're hired."

One month later, feeling confident, I headed for my "real interview." The fashion director was not too far into the interview when she told me she was losing her fashion coordinator, who was pregnant. She went on

NOW *or* NEVER

to say she had made up her mind that the next fashion coordinator would be a mature woman who wasn't going to get pregnant. There I was in living color, a perfect candidate.

At 2:30 on the same day, I received a call from the personnel director, saying, "I was hired." I was now a fashion coordinator for a large department store. Feeling joyous, I quit my job at the bookstore and stopped working for my friends. They were all happy for me and celebrated this major accomplishment with me. I learned some valuable lessons from my experiences, and probably the most important lesson was: *where I happened to be in my life was not the result of inferior abilities, but of an inferior opinion I had of myself.*

Joan Kennedy

Preface

We have incredible power and intelligence within us. It is constantly responding to our thoughts and words. We have the capacity to choose love, wealth, success, and happiness. Our mind will accept and bring to pass, in a natural way, whatever we assume and believe to be true.

This power, as well as every other power of nature, is in constant operation and is not concerned with us as individuals. It relentlessly gives us exactly what we create through our thoughts, words, feelings, and desires.

Our past thoughts are gone. There is nothing we can do about them except to live with the consequences. What we are thinking now is totally under our control. *This moment now* is our point of power!

NOW *or* NEVER

Your Power Source

To change the quality of our lives, we need to change the quality of our thinking.

Joan Kennedy

"You are what you think. You attract what you think. Your life is a product of your thoughts and beliefs, and nothing in the world can change this fact. To alter your life, the only course open to you, is to alter your thinking."

–James Allen.

These are simple words. They were not meant to confuse us. Through these words, we become aware that thought is a vital living force that we can use to mold and shape our lives.

Q: What will you do with this power now?

The law of thought
is as definite
as other laws of nature.

Joan Kennedy

An honest inventory of what we have in our everyday lives will give us a good idea of the thinking we have engaged in. The subconscious mind can bring us the things we desire, like success, confidence, love, and peace of mind. It can also bring us failure, frustration, fear, and self-doubt. Success, happiness, and a great future are all around us and can be ours, depending on what we think and say each day to ourselves and to others.

Q: **What have you been thinking and saying to yourself and to others?**

What thoughts are you
giving power to now?

Joan Kennedy

We have an incredible power within us. When we speak, think, or maintain a negative thought, such as:

- *Nothing seems to work out for me.*
- *Every time I get a little money ahead, something always happens.*
- *Everything happens to me. I just don't seem to get anywhere.*

It is essential that you consciously discard the negative phrases and thoughts, as they bring you the very opposite of what you want.

Q: Would you ask this power to create such conditions in your life?

Things happen in our mind before they can happen in our lives.

Joan Kennedy

When we accept life as it unfolds, one day at a time, without consciously taking control of our thoughts, we turn our life over to our mind's conditioning. Everything we experience is largely the result of our own thinking. To change our lives, we need to change our thinking.

Q: **Do you believe that the conditions under which you live are the result of your thoughts?**

Time is our most precious element, we cannot thoughtlessly let it slip away.

Joan Kennedy

Our past thoughts, words and beliefs brought us to this moment. What we choose to think, believe, and say, will create the next moment, the next day, the next month, and the years ahead. No one can prevent us from being successful, and happy, except ourselves. Our thoughts and our words create the picture of what we draw to ourselves.

Q: **Are you aware of the things you say, or think about, during the course of a day?**

NOW *or* NEVER

Our subconscious
mind responds
to habitual thinking.

Joan Kennedy

It's not the profound thought you have that affect you, it's the little repetitious thoughts you have each moment of every day. And it doesn't matter when or where the thought comes. It can come to you in the silence of your bedroom, or in the midst of a busy day. If you hold onto that thought, it will in time become a reality in your life.

Q: What are some of the habitual negative thoughts you entertain during the course of a day?

NOW *or* NEVER

Happiness, health, and success, are results—and these results are created by positive thinking.

Joan Kennedy

We are equipped with the necessary elements, qualities, and potential, to make our life the one we truly want to live. Success, happiness, and a great future are all around us, and can be ours, depending on what we think and say to ourselves and others each day.

Q: Do you remember the thoughts you had yesterday? Were they mostly positive?

Our negative pattern of thought binds us to lives of limitations and mediocrity.

Joan Kennedy

We limit ourselves by habitually thinking only of our small everyday occurrences. We don't allow ourselves to venture into the boundless realm where we can envision wonderful and more fulfilling experiences— believing that something can be done paves the way for creative solutions.

Q: **Can you envision great things happening to you?**

NOW *or* NEVER

It's at the Core of Your Being

A strong and positive
self-image is something everyone
needs.

Joan Kennedy

We all carry a mental picture of the kind of person we think we are. We acquire our self-image through our beliefs about ourselves, which grow out of past experiences of success and failure, and how we think others see us. Changing things in our lives is a matter of changing our beliefs about them.

Q: Do you believe that your self-image is your greatest asset—or your greatest liability?

NOW *or* NEVER

If we believe that we have no talent, or we are too old, and nobody wants us, these become our convictions, to be accepted by our mind and acted upon.

Page 40

Joan Kennedy

The limitations we feel, the goals we set for ourselves, our whole approach toward life, is strongly influenced by the image we have of ourselves. Once an idea about ourselves goes into this image, it becomes true, as far as we are concerned. We will act like the kind of person we think we are—we can't act any other way.

Q: Do you believe that you won't know who you really are until you deal with the person you think you are?

We all talk to ourselves,
whether we realize it or not.

Joan Kennedy

Through our inner dialogue we make decisions, set goals, feel pleased and satisfied, depressed or unfulfilled. As soon as we alter how we perceive ourselves, we begin to change. Changing our self-talk from negative to positive can be the first step in raising our self-image.

Q: **Does your inner dialogue play a key role in determining how you feel about yourself?**

We need to get rid of
the thoughts that
diminish us.

Joan Kennedy

You are never too old to change; creating a new self-image releases your talents and abilities. You have the power to do what you want to do. This power becomes available as soon as you change the beliefs you have of yourself. Focus on your strengths, not your weaknesses. If you underrate yourself, others are likely to do the same.

Q: Do you sometimes think you are less than others?

NOW *or* NEVER

When you raise
your self-image,
you raise your potential.

Joan Kennedy

It isn't who we are, it's who we think we are that sets the boundaries of our accomplishments. Our position in life is not the result of inferior abilities, but of inferior opinions we have of ourselves. We all have abilities we don't know about. We can do things we never dreamed we could do. It's usually only when necessity forces us that we rise to the occasion and do the things that seemed impossible before.

Q*:* **Do you tend to minimize the things you can accomplish?**

Regret serves no purpose,
other than to keep us
stuck in the past.

Joan Kennedy

Many of us carry the memory of past mistakes, and use the energy of the moment to review them. Whatever we did, or didn't do, we need to forgive ourselves. Letting go of the "I should have," "Why did I," "If only," serves no purpose in our lives today.

Q*:* **Are the thoughts you are thinking today the same thoughts you were thinking yesterday and the day before?**

NOW *or* NEVER

A Method of Change

An affirmation is a declaration of what you are or can be.

Joan Kennedy

Affirmations are like seeds planted in your mind, and given time, they will grow into your reality. It stands to reason that if your present situation is the result of past negative suggestions, you can reverse the pattern.

If you affirm, *I am disorganized*, you are making an undesired condition a reality. On the other hand, if you say, *I am well organized in all areas of my life*, you will eventually live up to those claims.

Q: Through affirmations, what changes would you like to make in your circumstances right now?

NOW *or* NEVER

Within us lies the cause of whatever enters our lives, and the effect is what we live with.

Joan Kennedy

Through affirmations we can raise our self-image, conquer our fears, and become self-confident. The subconscious mind is extremely receptive and can be convinced of any premise we present it, negative or positive, true or false. Unlike our conscious mind, our subconscious is impersonal.

It treats everything we say with the same indifference. It just accepts and obeys, and brings back to us the things we think about, talk about, and believe to be true.

Q: Through the power of affirmations, what change would you want to make in yourself?

To affirm is to state it is so, and as we maintain this attitude of mind as true, we will gradually change.

Joan Kennedy

If we want this powerful, creative mind to work in our favor, we need to stop giving it the wrong commands. The sub-conscious mind is so powerful, and so subject to suggestions, that in affirmations, we have a tool of extraordinary power. Through affirmations, we can make changes in ourselves, in our circumstances and in our lives.

Q: Through affirmation, what changes would you want to make in your life?

This present moment is your point of power, wherein you can change yourself and your life.

Joan Kennedy

If you consciously follow the method of daily affirmations, even for a short time, they will produce satisfying results in your life. The affirmation to achieve self-confidence is:

"I am completely relaxed and self-assured in all situations and with all people."

With confidence you will become more relaxed, more sure of your-self, and enjoy life more.

Q*:* **Do you think one of the surest ways to become confident is through affirmations, or are there other ways to become more confident?**

The moving force of
"I am, I have, I can,"
will bring dynamic
dimensions to your life.

Joan Kennedy

Affirmations can be said while sitting in a relaxed position. It is important to say each affirmation five times and in the present tense. Through affirmations, you can make changes in yourself and in your circumstances. You need to phrase your affirmations in the present tense, such as, "I am losing weight," rather than, "I'm going to lose weight." "Going to," is in the future. This moment "Now," is your point of power.

Q: Would you take the time to make daily affirmations if you believed they would change you and your life?

Listen more closely to others:
You'll find they have some of the
same doubts and fears as you do.

Joan Kennedy

One of the surest ways to become confident is through affirmations. When you are confident, it frees you of unnecessary worry and fear. People don't know how you feel, unless you send them messages that tell them you're not sure of yourself. Eye contact, and the way you walk, talk, and act often communicates these messages. Projecting confidence is being in control of the messages you send.

Q: **Are you in control of the messages you send to others?**

NOW *or* NEVER

Dream Big!
Think Big!
Set a Big Goal!

There is magic in thinking big. Thinking big is behind every successful business.

Joan Kennedy

Think Big! It's the driving force in all great accomplishments. The first step is to decide on a big goal. See yourself as the person who can achieve that goal. Concentrate on why you can do it, not why you can't. Whatever you truly believe you can do, can be done. Remember, you only have one life to live, don't waste it thinking you don't have what it takes.

Q: Do you have a major goal that you are working on now?

NOW *or* NEVER

We all start with the same number of hours in a day. It's what we do with the time that counts.

Joan Kennedy

If your goal is to be reached in a minimum of time, every day must count. "Now" is the word for success. Not tomorrow, next week, or someday. The more specific you can make your goal, the easier it is to focus. A clearly defined goal, backed by a burning desire, becomes a powerful combination.

Q: Do you have a burning desire to achieve your present goal?

Many of us go through life
without coming within sight
of a major goal.

Joan Kennedy

You have no real success in life until you act upon that which you feel will   fulfill you. If you don't, each birthday will serve as a reminder of lost opportunity. To have control over your life, you need to decide how you want to use your energies. The three qualities that separate people   who do things from people who merely think about doing them are: persistence, concentration, and passion.

Q: **What major goals do you want to accomplish in the next five years?**

Goals give purpose
to the way you spend
your days.

Joan Kennedy

One of the basic drives leading to achievement is a deep heartfelt purpose that gives you the strength to encounter adversity without allowing it to deplete your determination to reach a goal. *In other words, you don't quit.* It's important to give yourself a time frame. If you fail to consider the time factor, you may give up too soon.

Q: What above anything else do you want to do in your life?

Setting goals stimulates excitement, motivates your efforts, and delivers what you want.

Joan Kennedy

If you want to have control of your life, you will need to decide where to use your energies. You can get involved in many things each day, and you enjoy doing many things, but in order to be effective with your time, you need to narrow it down to things you really want, and be specific.

Q: Do you often say, "The things I do aren't necessarily the things I want to do?"

**Nothing happens until
we make a decision.**

Joan Kennedy

It is this inability to make a decision as to what we want to do that keeps us from acting. To make any changes, to accomplish any task, we have to come to a decision. It is vitally important to make a decision, but until we act, it remains a matter of, "I would like to." We all start out with the same amount of minutes in a day. It's what we do with them that count. Take action, and something will happen.

Q: Is it easy for you to make a decision and then to take immediate action?

Stop thinking about how
to start, just start.

Joan Kennedy

Often, we get caught up in a mental trap of seeing enormously successful people, and thinking they are where they are because they have some kind of gift we don't have.

The greatest gift that successful people have over the average person, is their ability to take action. Having made a decision, don't waste time reviewing it. Act on your decision. Do something, no matter how simple.

Q: Do you make excuses for not doing something, or do you take immediate action?

The more you deliberate on the best way to get started, the less likely you are to get started.

Joan Kennedy

Planning is vitally important in getting results, but it can never be a substitute for action. Any decision you make will not be firm until you act on it, and the longer you put off doing something, the shakier your decision becomes. When you finally decide to act, you not only jumpstart your life, you give it direction.

Q: Do you have a tendency to wait until conditions are just right before you act?

NOW *or* NEVER

Concentration is focusing attention on your goal, and refusing to consider anything that is not pertinent to your objective.

Joan Kennedy

To succeed in life, to do the things we want to do, to have the things we want to have, we must focus on what we want, not on what we don't have. And if we are to reach our goal in a minimum of time, every day must count. Keep in mind, we don't have to do everything today, but we have to do something every day.

Q: **Do you work on one task every day that pertains to your major goal?**

NOW *or* NEVER

Keep your mind on your goal,
not on the obstacles.

Joan Kennedy

The Shop at The Marsh

15000 Minnetonka Boulevard
Minnetonka, MN, 55345
P: 952-930-8525 F: 952-930-8551

The Marsh

Receipt   **04/12/2018- 3:27 pm**

Guest, Marsh   Folio: **251536**

Printed By: Tren D (763)

Item	Price	Disc	Qty	Ext. Price
Book Now or Never 192684	14.95	0	1	14.95
		Subtotal		14.95

Discount Summary:

Discount Total		**(0.00)**
Henn. Cty. Sales Tax		0.10
MN State Sales Tax		1.03
Total		**$ 16.08**
Payments		**$ 16.08**
Balance		**$ 0.00**

Payment	Notes	Date	Amount
VISA	ROUSSEAU/ JUDY	12-Apr-2018	16.08

www.themarsh.com

Printed On: 04/12/2018- 3:27 pm

The Marsh

Receipt	04/12/2018 3:27 pm
Guest: Marsh	Folio 251536

Printed By: Tran D (763)

Item	Qty	Disc (s)	Price
Base Towel 16 x 27 264	1	0.00	14.99

Subtotal 14.99

Discount Summary

Discount Total (0.00)

Minn City Sales Tax 0.16
Minn State Sales Tax 1.03

Total	$ 16.08
Payments	$ 16.08
Balance	$ 0.00

Payment - Visa	Date	Amount
VISA	AMX FS/00 LTD	12-Apr-2018 16:28

The Shop at The Marsh
15000 Minnetonka Boulevard
Minnetonka,MN
US
55345

952-930-8525

Merchant #:   322958
Invoice #:   7000243552

Bus. type: POS
Folio #:   251536
Staff #:   763

4/12/2018   15:27:04

Card #:   ***********8110
Card type: VISA

Transaction: Purchase
Total: 16.08

Reference #:   092676

       *** Purchase - Success ***

_____
Signature

Cardholder will pay card issuer above
amount pursuant to Cardholder Agreement.

              Merchant Copy

952-930-6323

Merchant #:	327394
Invoice #:	200024595?
Sale type:	POS
Folio #:	281836
Clerk #:	083

8/17/2018   15:27:04

Card #:	************0110
Card Type:	VISA
Transaction:	Purchase
Total:	$1.08
Reference #:	092676

*** Purchase - Success ***

_____
Signature

Successful living does not come to only those who are the brightest, youngest, or the most knowledgeable. A life that is successful is achieved by those who are dedicated, determined, and never gave up. So it isn't what you think about, talk about, or plan to do— it's what you actually do each day that determines your future.

Q: **Do you think the difference between success and failure hinges on whether you do something today—or do it tomorrow?**

There is no purpose
or vitality without goals.

Joan Kennedy

If you don't consciously choose how you will spend your time on this earth, you lose it to the nonessential tasks, or in spending your time meeting other people's needs.

If you can be selective in saying yes, and comfortable with saying no, you will have the time and energy to do what it is you want to do in this lifetime.

Q: Do you find yourself spending time on other people's need?

Fear Stops You in Your Tracks

Each day's choices will
determine the quality of your life.

Joan Kennedy

Fear and faith are the greatest factors competing for control of your mind, especially when setting goals.

- Fear is a powerful force. It keeps you from asserting yourself.
- Fear steals your confidence, and persuades you to set easier goals.
- Fear keeps you from being the person you were meant to be.
- Fear keeps you from taking the risks necessary for changing your life.

Q: **What is your number one fear?**

NOW *or* NEVER

Fear prevents us
from accomplishing
our goals.

Joan Kennedy

The two most common fears are: the fear of failure, and the fear of criticism. We usually bring past failures into our consciousness when we're working on a new goal. Instead of envisioning ourselves succeeding, we remember our failures, and as we give them energy, with our thoughts, we give them life. By thinking of past failures we are, in truth, reliving them and making them our present.

Q: *What does your number one fear keep you from doing?*

NOW *or* NEVER

Every day thousands of people bury good ideas because they are afraid to act on them.

Joan Kennedy

We've all had inspired moments when we see clearly how we can do a certain thing, but we don't have enough confidence in ourselves, or our idea, to make it a reality. Then, sooner or later, someone else comes along who has no more ability or background, and does the very thing we had envisioned for ourselves. The fear of criticism can bring on a lack of initiative, and a lack of ambition, because it creates a feeling of self-doubt. No philosophy will help us achieve anything, if we doubt our abilities to do so.

Q: What do you put off doing because of your number one fear?

Fear is the number one enemy of success.

Joan Kennedy

No matter how hard you work for success, if your thoughts are filled with the fear of failure, it will paralyze your efforts. Fear, will keep you from being assertive and going for what you really desire. The potential for achievement exists within you. Nothing can stop you except your own doubts and fears. Each time you experience success, it instills further confidence in you, which in turn, breeds more confidence. Confidence is the ingredient in self-assurance, and the conviction that you can deal successfully with life and its challenges.

Q: **Have you ever decided not to follow through with a good idea because of your doubts and fears?**

NOW *or* NEVER

Forget the failures of yesterday and fears of tomorrow for they don't exist. Think of today and achieve something today.

Joan Kennedy

Whenever we do something new, we feel the fear—and being uncomfortable is enough reason for us not to do something. We also experience fear when we are on unfamiliar territory, *but so does everyone else.* When people look back on their lives, they regret actions and risks not taken, far more than the mistakes they made, even the big ones. The only way to get rid of the fear of doing something is to go out and do it. The time to act is now.

Q: When you have the urge to do something, do you act on it now, or put it off until later?

NOW *or* NEVER

Visualize What You Want

Only you can
create for yourself,
what you want.

Joan Kennedy

Decide now what it is you want in life—exactly what you wish your future to be. Visualize each step along the way. Create a detailed image of yourself as you will be when you get what you desire. See yourself now, doing those things you have always wanted to do and have. Make them real in your mind's eye. When you picture the way you really want your life to be, you improve your chances of achieving your dreams.

Q: Do you have a firm belief that you are your own power source?

When we achieve a feeling   of confidence, through affirmations and our creative visualization, we will notice a change in the attitude of the people around us.

Joan Kennedy

Visualization is not fantasy. It is creating a real situation in the future, and then seeing yourself in that situation. All the things that are now your reality were once simply ideas in your consciousness. Create your own positive images of yourself, and make room for new things in your life.

Albert Einstein said, *"Your imagination is, your preview of life's coming attraction."* Visualization is seeing in your mind's eye conditions or circumstances not as they are—but as you want them to be.

Q: Do you think that what you picture in your mind will manifest in your life?

The difference
between people
is the difference in vision.

Joan Kennedy

*A*nything that has been accomplished has first been created and imagined in your mind. Create your own positive image of yourself, and for new things in your life.

First there is the vision, then the accomplishment. In order to grow, develop, and achieve, you must accept the subconscious way to do it. With this power to call upon, there is no problem too difficult to overcome.

Q: Do you make a habit of visualizing the goals you want to achieve?

The only moment
we can live in,
is this present moment.

Joan Kennedy

It is necessary to visualize the things we would like to see in our lives. It's important to forget about the negative things that happened to us in the past. In place of them, we need to mentally create the conditions we would like to see now. How many of us are excited about life this moment, rather than living in that nebulous time we call someday, when we have more money, more time, more love, and more fun?

Q: Have you ever said to yourself: I can't picture myself doing that?

A Self-fulfilling Prophesy

At every age, your life deserves fulfillment, meaning, fun, and laughter.

Joan Kennedy

Many of us are apprehensive about growing older, because it could mean the loss of status, personal effectiveness, youth, attractiveness, and the possible loss of health. We continue to accept the outdated ideas of aging, and consequently create for ourselves a negative image of our own aging. Good reasons why we can live long lives: good health, good nature, good connections with family and friends, and good thoughts about growing older.

Q: **What are some of the beliefs you have about growing older?**

We create our own emptiness
when we just drift.

Joan Kennedy

As we grow older, it's important to have something in our future to look forward to, to aspire to. If we don't, we will come to a point in our lives when we begin to look to the past and view that time as the time we did all our living.

We see it all around us, men and women who have grown old with no new goals or dreams, only memories of what they did, and who they used to be. The quickest way to grow old is to stop setting goals.

Q: What can you do now to stay in the mainstream of life?

NOW *or* NEVER

To age well is to stay healthy.

Joan Kennedy

One of the things we must do is to protect the health we now have. Without our health, there is very little we can do or look forward to. With our health we have options: we can work, be productive, be socially active, have relationships, travel, and set and achieve our goals. The goal for all of us is a life of productivity, good health, fun, and laughter.

Q: **What are you doing to protect the health you now have?**

NOW *or* NEVER

No one else is going to come along to make your life more than it is. Your life is an individual responsibility, an individual opportunity, and an individual experience.

Joan Kennedy

As long as you live, you have the privilege of growth. You can learn new skills, engage in new kinds of work, meet new people, and have new relationships. The greatest relationship you will ever have is the relationship you have with yourself. You will never leave you. You will never divorce you. You will never die on you. It's time to promise to love, honor, and cherish yourself, and be your own best friend.

Q: Do you love, honor and cherish yourself...now?

Everything changes,
based on how
we perceive it.

Joan Kennedy

We have learned in a hundred ways to revere what is young and dislike what is old. In our culture focused on youth, we've been forced to see each birthday, after seventy, as a harbinger of lost youth, vitality, attractiveness, strength, and sexuality. We need to listen to our bodies, mind, and instincts—not to what our neighbors or friends may think or say.

Q: Are you anxious or fearful about growing older?

Life is too short,
too wonderful, to live in fear of
growing older.

Joan Kennedy

Nothing could be more destructive to the human spirit than the idea there are no more dreams, no more challenges, no more new and enjoyable experiences. Life has more to offer for those of us who are willing to plan our own adventures and create our own joys. In fact, as long as we live, there isn't a set date or line in the sand that says, "We're finished."

Q: **What can you change within yourself and in your future, now?**

Life is dynamic, it's
never static.

Joan Kennedy

We are always in the process of growth. There is always room for creative thought, new options, and new discoveries, as long as we live. Age has less to do with years than it has to do with our attitude. It's up to us to take a realistic view of ourselves to determine the opportunities that are ahead of us, in the future.

Q: **What activities can you become involved in to stay motivated and stimulated?**

For those willing to plan their own adventure, and create their own joy, life has more to offer.

Joan Kennedy

I t's up to you to take a realistic view of yourself, and to consider what you need to do to ensure that your future will be productive, fulfilling, and satisfying. The antidote for aging is action. Whatever dreams you once had for yourself, bring them back. They may be even more exciting the second time around. Emerson said, *"If we did all the things we were capable of doing, we would literally astound ourselves."*

Q: What have you always wanted to do and experience?

No one knows for certain how old someone has to be to be old.

Joan Kennedy

We continue to accept outdated ideas of aging, and consequently create for ourselves a negative image of our own aging. We need to remember that our attitude about aging is the most crucial factor in our adjustment to it. There is more to being young than simply being pretty or being free of wrinkles, gray hair, and age spots. People who are young have inquisitive minds; they are curious and ready to try something new. They enjoy themselves and have fun.

Q: What is your attitude about your own aging?

Taking a positive view of your own aging is the only sane decision you can make.

Joan Kennedy

Taking hold of your present moment is one of the steps to living happily, not postponing your pleasures until someday. Many of us play the game of "I'll be happy" when I get my bills paid, when the report is finished, when the house is painted, when I get on top of things." If you thought for a moment that you only had six months to live, what would be the most important thing you would want to do, to finish, to leave behind?

Q: What are some of the most important things you want to do…now?

Tomorrow isn't promised to anyone. Do it now!

Joan Kennedy

The things we wish we had done in our lives will be the things we put off, the dreams we let slip away, relationships we failed to nurture, and projects we started but never finished. Make a decision now to celebrate our lives, and put into it every day love, learning, adventure, and pleasure whenever we can. And not to forget to tell our family and friends how much we love them, as often as we can.

Q: **What are some of the things you want to stop putting off…now?**

About the Author

Joan Kennedy is a well-known speaker and author. She was a stay-at-home mom for eighteen years, and at age forty-five, she went back to work as a fashion coordinator for  a large department store. At fifty she became a motivational speaker.

For two years, she presented daily motivational and inspirational messages on an East Coast radio station.

Joan published her first book at age fifty-six: *I Don't Want Much from Life, I Want More.* At eighty-three she published, *What's Age Got to Do with It?* She compiled stories from forty women for the book, *Unlocking the Secrets of Successful Women*, which became an Amazon Best Seller. At ninety-four she compiled stories from thirty-two women for the book, *Women of a Certain Age.*

Her true passion is helping women to become more confident and empowered. Her message to them is, "You only have one

NOW *or* NEVER

life to live, don't waste it thinking you don't have what it takes."

Joan has spread her philosophy through books and speaking engagements. She has worked with corporations, health care organizations, conventions, conferences, and women of all ages.

Today at 95, Joan bills herself as the oldest motivational speaker in the country.

joan@joankennedy.com
www.joankennedy.com

Joan Kennedy

Book Order Form

NOW or NEVER

The Choice is Yours

Price

$14.95 (tax included)

$3.00 Shipping

Send $17.95 to:

Joan Kennedy

602 Edgemoor Drive

Hopkins, MN 55305

Email: joan@joankennedy.com

www.joankennedy.com

Name_____

Address _____

City _____State_____Zip _____

Phone Number _____

Email _____

Quantity of Books _____@ $_____ **each**

Total $_____

Shipping & handling $3

Each additional book shipping charge $3

Total $_____

Make checks out to Joan Kennedy.

Every day, in every way I AM healthier & healthier.